CHIEKO'S SKY

CHIEKO'S

SKY

Kotaro TAKAMURA

translated by Soichi FURUTA

illustrated by Chieko TAKAMURA

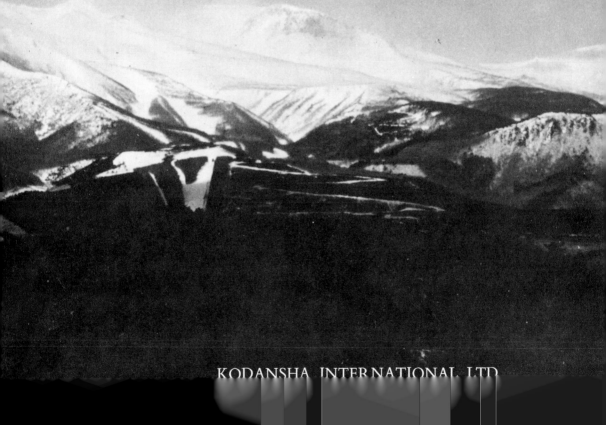

KODANSHA INTERNATIONAL LTD

Publication of this book was assisted by a grant from the Japan Foundation.

This is a revised edition of *Chieko-sho: Poems for Chieko*, published in 1974 by Mushinsha, Tokyo, and Grossman Publishers, New York.

Distributed in the United States by Kodansha International/USA, Ltd., through Harper & Row, Publishers, Inc., 10 East 53rd Street, New York, New York 10022; in Canada by Fitzhenry & Whiteside Limited, 150 Lesmill Road, Don Mills, Ontario; in Mexico and Central America by HARLA S.A. de C.V., Apartado 30-546, Mexico 4, D.F.; in South America by Harper & Row, International Department; in the United Kingdom by Phaidon Press Ltd., Littlegate House, St. Ebbe's Street, Oxford OX1 1SQ; in Continental Europe by Boxerbooks Inc., Limmatstrasse 111, 8031 Zurich; in Australia and New Zealand by Book Wise (Australia) Pty. Ltd., 104-8 Sussex Street, Sydney 2000; in the Far East by Toppan Company (S) Pte. Ltd., Box 22 Jurong Town Post Office, Jurong, Singapore 22.

Published by Kodansha International Ltd., 2-12-21 Otowa, Bunkyo-ku, Tokyo 112 and Kodansha International/USA, Ltd., 10 East 53rd Street, New York, New York 10022 and 44 Montgomery Street, San Francisco, California 94104. Copyright © 1978 by Kodansha International Ltd. All rights reserved. Printed in Japan.
First edition, 1978   JBC 1092-786043-2361

Library of Congress Cataloging in Publication Data

Takamura, Kotaro, 1883–1956.
  Chieko's sky.

  Translation of Chieko-sho.
  1. Takamura, Chieko Naganuma, 1886–1938—Poetry.
I. Title.
PL817.A43C513 1978   895.6′1′4   77-75970
ISBN 0-87011-313-5

N.B. Except on the cover and title page, all Japanese names are given in the Japanese order—surname first, followed by the given name.

*This translation is dedicated
to my deceased mother,
Misao, and Yoshiya.*

contents

translator's preface

forming is Nature's axis.
sine qua non of the world's existence.
from "To play with Chieko"

Kotaro was a sculptor, first of all.
He sculpted his poetry with a sculptor's hands.
Hands.
Certainly not merely with a painter's eyes.
His poetry was a "body" poetry, tactile and immediate.
As "body" equates with "form" in sculpture,
his was a "form" poetry. He did not write poems,
he formed them.
Thus in "Naked form" he wrote:

> I long for the naked form of Chieko.
> modest and full
> solemn like a constellation
> undulating like a mountain range
> always covered with thin mist
> there was a fathomless sheen
> to its agatelike formation.
>
> . . . .
>
> to create that formation once again
> with my hands
> is a covenant fixed by nature.

In his poem "You get prettier and prettier,"
he sculpts the woman Chieko's body. . . .

> your body washed by age
> is heavenly metal flying through infinity.

Brancusi once said,
"My hands think and follow the thoughts of my materials."
So did Kotaro's hands think and follow
the thoughts of his materials
—his wife Chieko, her body and soul together.

Chieko became his "particular" universe,
with which he tried to be one.
Basho once said,

>Go to the pine if you would learn about the pine.
>When you and the object have become one,
>Your poetry issues of its own accord.

So Kotaro went to Chieko to learn about Chieko
and become one with Chieko.
And his poems flowed out of him
of their own accord.
This is his poetics.
Many love poems have been written,
but none like Chieko's Sky,
this forty-year chronicle
of one man's love affair with a singular woman.
Many erotic poems have been written.
"The Song of Songs," Catullus, Villon,
Shakespeare, Byron, Heine, Baudelaire,
Lawrence, Eliot, Cummings, Neruda....
Despite stylistic variations
in terms of romantic euphemism, bawdiness, symbolism, and so on,
the underlying keynote was always an "ambiguous eroticism,"
in which the object of love was never revealed
as explicitly as Chieko was.
Kotaro wrote a hymn of the body, a critic has said,
candid, bold, and tender,
almost in the tradition of Walt Whitman who sang:

>Of physiology from top to toe I sing,
>Not physiognomy alone nor brain alone is worthy for the
>   Muse, I say the Form complete is worthier far,
>The Female equally with the Male I sing.

Here in Chieko's Sky *the Form complete of Chieko*
is laid bare for us by the fierce hands

of Kotaro the sculptor.
Love has seldom been etched more concretely
and vitally as in "a salamander dances violently"
in his poem "In admiration of love."
There have also been many painter-poets or poet-painters,
like Wang Wei, Buson, Blake, Hesse, and Klee.
Since Michelangelo, however, there has been
no sculptor-poet of major stature
but Kotaro.
He was neither a sculptor who dabbled in poetry
nor a poet who dabbled in sculpture.
In Japan, his place as the father of both
modern sculpture and modern poetry
has long been established.
Pursuing that "heavenly metal flying through infinity,"
Kotaro struggled to enter Chieko's world of
absolute reality.

> Chieko is in dimension a.
> dimension a is absolute reality.
> . . . .
> all is a playful stroll over Chieko's dimension a.
> as we play, we get a little less vulgar.

It is with these last lines
of Kotaro's in mind
that I would like to give this translation
of a unique volume of love
to the Western reader.

to someone

just can't stand
your going away.........

like bearing fruit before flowering
like budding before seeding
like spring coming right out of summer
please don't do
such an absurd unnatural thing
just the thought of a stereotyped husband
and you who write in a round hand
is enough to make me cry
getting married? why you—
you who are timid like a bird
capricious as a great wind?

just can't stand
your going away.........

how could you so easily
how shall I say?... well...
feel like selling yourself?
yes, selling yourself
from the world of one
to the world of everyone
yielding yourself, so senselessly yielding
yourself to the man
oh, what a hideous act!
like a Titian
out shopping in Times Square
I am lonely   I am sad
uncertain
it's like watching that fat Gloxinia

you gave me
rotting
like seeing it degenerate, deserting me
like staring at the trace of a bird
traveling through the sky
it's that sad desperate feeling of a broken surge
fleeting   lonely   burning
. . . yet it's different from love
Santa Maria
nothing like that   nothing like that
though I don't know why, to begin with. . . . .
just can't stand
your going away. . . . .
much less, your getting married
yielding to another man's whim

July, 1912

heart of one night

look, the moon of a July night
running a fever in the poplar grove
a faint waft of fragrance from cyclamen
sobbing on your silent lips
woods, roads, grass and distant streets
writhing in a causeless sorrow
and heaving white sighs faintly
a young couple holding hands side by side
treading over the black soil
an invisible demon draining a sweet wine
an echo of the earth-rumbling last train
sounding like a mockery of man's fate
my soul has secretly begun to writhe
moistening a sash of Indian chintz with sweat
trying to maintain the patience of a fire worshiper
heart, heart
wake up, my heart
wake up, your heart
what can this mean?
inseparable, painful, inescapable
and sweet, hard to leave, unbearable
heart, heart
rise from the sickbed
abandon the hashish doze
everything visible, though, now seems maddening
look, even the moon of a July night
running a fever in the poplar grove
incurable illness
my heart tormented by beautiful vermin
on the grass of a greenhouse
heart, heart
. . . what, alas, are you calling now
in this silent midnight?

August, 1912

fear

you mustn't   you mustn't
put your hands on this tranquil water
much less, toss in a stone
even the single tremor of one waterdrop
would waste a myriad of useless ripples
you must revere the stillness of water
and measure the value of silence

you mustn't tell me more
what you're about to say is so damned perilous
better not to speak
if spoken, then it's a thunder fire
you are a woman
after all, a woman, though they say you are manlike
you are that round moon sweating in the blue-black sky
that moon leading the world to a dream
                    and transposing an instant to eternity
enough   enough
don't bring the dream back to reality
and eternity back to the instant
much less
toss such a perilous thing
into this limpid water

the stillness of my mind is a treasure bought by blood
the treasure that sacrificed blood incomprehensible to you
this stillness is my life
this stillness is my god
moreover, a fastidious god
who threatens even now to disrupt
the appetite of a summer night
would you dare touch that very spot?

you must   you must
you must measure the value of silence
or else
set to work with extraordinary resolution
the ripple stirred by that single stone
might assault you and engulf you in the whirlpool
might shock you a hundred thousand times harder
you are a woman
you must foster strength enough to bear this
but can you do it, I wonder
you mustn't tell me more
you mustn't   you mustn't

look
isn't this smoggy, greasy station
now like a treasure-house shrouding some great beauty
in this moon and a little sultry mist?
that green and red signal is playing
a tremendous role between silence and glancing
and tuning up the moon-night emotion far away
now, surrounded by something
a certain atmosphere
a certain formless power governing a strange modulation
I am poised in most precious balance
my soul musing on eternity
my eyes finding infinite value in all things
quietly   quietly
keeping in touch with an unknown force
am I now forgetting a language

you mustn't   you mustn't
put your hands on this tranquil water
much less, toss in a stone

August, 1912

peep-show song

(in praise of the very innocent tableaux of a peep show)

the Deep North is the country
                    the Twin Pines is the village
watch her run
across the red-brick wine cellar
that woman, fleeing
a woman just like wine
born suddenly out of wine froth
her destination was Kichijoji
that would burn down anyway
even the River Abukuma's water
could never douse this fire
together, wine and water
are true foes
wine and water indeed!

                              August, 1912

one evening

fire burning in a gas stove
oolong tea, wind, thin evening moon

... that's it, yes, that's the world
the sincerity they covet is nothing but a dress uniform
it's a masquerade of nature
it's the erect position of attention
in the confusion of the world they have lost their minds
—the minds of the self-knowing that had once been naked
don't be surprised
that's the world
a gang of abominable, cruel men
harboring vulgar thoughts
and staring an inch before their eyes
and so the man who endeavors to live true
... as it was in the beginning, is now, and ever shall be ...
is, on the contrary, judged insincere
suffers persecution as you suffered
those cowards
and hypocrites
first look at us with voices of wonder
then sing the gamut of abuse, to while away their time
for they, the insincere, just meddle with events
                    and disregard the persons concerned
to be contemptible is the world
to be shameful is a little man involved in it
doing what we are born to do
advancing on the right path
respecting the laws of nature
we must reach a land where our thoughts are always
                    in harmony with natural law

the best power comes only from belief in ourselves
don't be surprised by their ugliness, like frogs
rather find in them beauty of the grotesque
to appreciate our loving hearts is enough
we must live in nature and freedom
breaking up all entanglements
like wind-blowing   like cloud-floating
if there is no falsehood in natural law, inner need,
                    and the promptings of wisdom, then it's good
nature is intelligent
nature is prudent
don't be vexed by those freaks
come now, let's eat a simple meal again in Ginza

October, 1912

to a woman in the suburbs

my heart now faces you like a gale
my love
piercing the blue fish skin, the cold night now deepens
so sleep peacefully at your suburban home
you are nothing but a child's sincerity
you are so purely transparent
all seeing you abandon malice
both good and evil stand exposed before you
you are truly the supreme judge
with a child's sincerity
you discovered my invaluable true self
in my numerous guises quite defiled
I know not what you found
only that when you are the supreme judge
my heart is rejoiced by you
my warm flesh is filled
with this self unknown to myself
it is winter, so the zelkova tree is bare
a soundless night
my heart now faces you like a gale
gushes out of the ground like a hot spring, soft and precious
immersing all your immaculate skin
though my heart jumps leaps romps
as you move along
it never forgets to protect you
my love
this is a peerless sacred font of life
so sleep peacefully
for it is a cold villainous winter night
sleep peacefully now at your suburban home
sleep like a child

November, 1912

winter morning awakening

it is a winter morning
so the River Jordan must be thinly frozen
shrouded in a white blanket, I am in my bedroom
I seek in my mind
the mind of John baptizing Christ
the mind of Salome holding the head of John
it is a winter morning, so from the streets
you'll hear the modest clatter of wooden clogs
let immense Nature be in my body's hold
let me walk
like a quietly revolving constellation
then the intense aroma of mocha
wide-eyed like the risen Spirit
steals into the chamber from somewhere
and I realize then
with almost mathematical detachment
what strange rhythm is pulsing in human society
rise my love
it is a winter morning
so a bulbul will come early to your suburban home singing
you'll have just opened your black eyes, my love
will stretch out your hands like a baby
will enjoy the morning light
and smile at the birds' voices
thinking thus
I am moved by an unbearable force

beating the white blanket
I sing a hymn of love
it is a winter morning
so my spirit stirs up joyfully
cries out loud
and thinks of a clean strong life
in the blue-amber sky
there drifts invisible gold dust
far away a pointer's barking
rouses my habit of pursuing things
and suddenly I yearn again for you, my love
it is a winter morning
so I shall bite the ice in the River Jordan

November, 1912

to someone

neither diversion
nor leisure
you come to see me
. . . no painting, no reading, no working . . .
and for two days, three days, even
we laugh, romp, jump and embrace
shorten our time ruthlessly
exhaust a few days in a moment

yes!
it's neither diversion
nor leisure
but our brimming inevitable lives
it's life
it's strength
abundance of August nature
seemingly extravagant, wasteful
lush grasses flowering and decaying deep in that mountain
sunlight crying out
cloud masses endlessly moving
abundant thunderclaps
rain and water
green, red, blue, and yellow
energy bursting out in the world
how can you see these things as a waste?
you dance for me
I sing for you

each and every moment of our lives we walk fully
the I at the moment of throwing a book away
and the I at the moment of opening a book
are the same in quantity
don't mistake in me
a vacuous diligence
for empty indolence
when your loving heart bursts
you come to see me
abandoning all, transcending all
trampling down all
and joyfully

February, 1913

midnight snow

a faint rustle of fire
in the warm gas stove
electric light in the closed study
shining quietly on a slightly tired couple
the sky cloudy since nightfall turns to snow
though it was already white all over
as we looked out of the window a short while ago
we felt the weight of snow soundlessly piling
on the ground, the roof, and our hearts
the world stares breathlessly in childlike wonder
at this soft weight covering joy
"hey look, it's already piled up so high!"
I hear a blurred voice from a distance
and the sound of snow being tapped off wooden clogs
then as the silent night nears eleven
all conversation gone
and the black tea tasting weary
just holding hands
we listen to the deep heart of this voiceless world
and stare at the figure of time drifting away
our faces faintly glistening, tranquil
we try to respond to everyone's feelings with ease
then again after the sound of snow-tapping
comes the hum of something like a car..........
as I say
"look! look at the snow"
my listener steps into a fairy tale
parts her lips
rejoices at the snow
the snow rejoices at the dead of night
and keeps falling down down down endlessly
the warm snow
the heavy snow deeply deeply bearing down on my body..........

February, 1913

14

us

whenever I think of you
I feel eternity most intimately
I am   you are
nothing more am I
my life and yours
twist   entangle   dissolve
and return to their chaotic origins
between us, every distinction becomes worthless
to us, all is absolute
there is no "man-woman strife"
only faith, devotion, love and freedom
and tremendous force and authority
a fusion of human polarities
I believe in our lives with the same ease
as I trust in Nature
and trample the world underfoot
I conquer the stubborn way of the world
we two ride far above
I feel my own pain as if it were yours
I feel my own pleasure as if it were yours
I rely upon you just as myself
I feel my own growth as your growth
I believe I'll never leave you behind
                    no matter how fast I walk, and feel easy
just as I am full of vitality
you gleam with youth
you are fire
you make me feel newer and newer as you get older and older
to me, you are the inexhaustibility of the new
you are reality, so sheer and whole
your kisses moisten me
your embraces nourish me
your cool limbs

your heavy, round body
your phosphorescent skin
the animal force piercing your whole body
all these become my finest nourishment
you depend on me
you live in me
all these mean to let you live
we prize our lives
we don't rest
we can't help rising high   infinitely high
we can't help growing
we can't help growing   infinitely big
we can't help growing   infinitely deep
. . . . .what light   what joy

December, 1913

in admiration of love

bottomless carnal desire
is a dreadful force on the flow. . . . .
in the sweaty fire still burning up
a salamander dances violently

the snow unceasing makes a feast vol-nuptial in the dead of night
cries up a joy in the desolate air
crushed down by an incredibly beautiful force
and now, immersing ourselves in a stream of profound mystery
breathing in the rosy mist stirred up
reflecting on the jewels of Indra's net
we mold our lives inexhaustibly

magic power of a cradle hidden in winter
and living heat of underground budding in winter. . . . .
that something burning inside all throbs together with the pulse of TIME
reverberates through our whole bodies with an electric current of ecstasy

our skins awaken wildly
our entrails writhe with the joy of life
hairs emit fluorescence
fingers creep all around the body discharging unique vitality
the true world of chaos possessing the Way
suddenly reveals its shape over us all

full of light
full of bliss
all distinctions wheel in unison

poison and nectar dwell in the same chest
unbearable ache contorts the body
ultimate ecstasy illuminates an enigmatic maze

warmly buried beneath the snow
dissolved in the elemental core of nature
devouring endless earthly love
we praise our lives far far away

February, 1914

supper

drenched
in a heavy downpour driven by storm
I bought a pound of rice
that cost me $24\frac{1}{2}$ cents
five dried mackerel
a piece of salted radish
red pickled ginger
eggs from the chicken coops
dried laver like hammered steel
fried fish cakes
soused bonitos

scalding water
we devour our supper like hungry demons

the storm gets worse
blasts the roof tiles
rattles and shakes the house
our appetite grows stronger and stronger
urged on by the instinct to create new blood
and soon we feel the bliss of satiety
hold hands quietly
cry the endless joy within our hearts
and pray
let life be in the trivia of each day
let minute brilliance be in the details of living
let the overflow be in us all
let us always be full

our supper
bears a more violent force than the storm
our after-supper fatigue
awakens in us a strange carnal passion
makes us marvel at our whole bodies
flaming up in the downpour

this is our supper, the supper of the poor

April, 1914

beneath the trees

that's Mt. Atatara,
that glistening there the River Abukuma.

as we sit quietly like this,
only the rustle of pine trees from long ago
blows dim-green through our somnolent heads.
let's stop hiding from that white cloud that looks down
on the joy of holding hands, burning quietly
amid these vast fields and mountains of early winter.
burning a strange elixir in the urn of your soul,
oh! to what a mysterious sea-bed of love you tempt me.
the panorama of the ten seasons we walked together
only reveals to me the feminine infinite within you.
that something smoldering in infinite space
purifies me, suffering intensely from desire,
and pours a fresh spring of youth on me,
                          burdened with so much bitterness.
it is elusive, like a specter,
and strangely protean.

that's Mt. Atatara,
that glistening there the River Abukuma.

this is your birthplace,
those tiny dots the white walls of your family's wine cellar.
let's stretch our legs then
and this endlessly clear day breathe the air full of
                          the tree-scent of the north.

let's bathe our skin in this atmosphere,
slim, elastic, and coolly pleasant just like yourself.
I am again going far away tomorrow
to that roguish metropole, the chaotic whirlpool of love and hatred,
right back into that human comedy I am afraid of but so attached to.
this is your birthplace,
world that bore this strange and singular body.
the pine trees are still rustling;
tell me once more the geography of
                    this lonely, early winter panorama.

that's Mt. Atatara,
that glistening there the River Abukuma.

                                        March, 1923

stampede

ah, so frightened you look,
you must have seen that now,
that herd of cattle charging madly on,
like demons passing by,
rumbling along the cypress forest of this deep mountain,
stirring up an avalanche in this distant, desolate territory
but now gone somewhere far away.

let's break up for today.
over the triangular shoulder of Mt. Hotaka that I've begun to paint
the earth-green clouds have already appeared.
the looming mountains dominate
the River Azusa, cerulean,
carrying down the thawing ice of Mt. Yari.
far off in the valley the wind bends the poplars.
let's stop painting for today
and make our favorite bonfire once again,
but careful not to desecrate this divine untrodden garden.
so come sit quietly
on this moss swept clean by Nature.

such fear as yours must come
from seeing that bloody, young, transfigured bull
dreadfully panting in pursuit
of the herd of cows, thundering on their way.
but the time will come when you too feel pity
for that blunt bestiality on this sacred mountain,
with much deeper knowledge of the world,
some day, smiling with love, serene..........

June, 1925

catfish

a splash in the basin.
as night deepens, a chill pierces the blade.
tree-whittling is the task of the north wind in the winter night.
catfish!
even if we run out of coals for the fireplace,
would you rather be devouring some enormous dream beneath the ice?
the chips of cypress wood are my kin,
Chieko is not afraid of poverty.
catfish!
what a fascinating salute to my work
is the sword in your fins,
tentacles in your tail,
blackish gold rings in your gills,
and such a stone head despite your optimism.
as the wind stills, the wooden floor breathes the scent of orchids.
Chieko has fallen asleep.
pushing the half-chiseled catfish aside,
moistening the stone again,
I swiftly whet a sharper blade for tomorrow.

February, 1926

a couple at night

a prophecy that our end will be
                death from starvation
was made by the sleety night rain
                falling on the snow.
though Chieko is a woman of
                extraordinary resolution
she has a medieval dream of preferring
                burning at the stake to death by starvation.
all remaining silent, once again
                we listened to the rain.
it's getting a little windy perhaps, rose branches are
                scratching at the windowpane.

March, 1926

you get prettier and prettier

when women cast off accessories one by one
why is it they become so beautiful?
your body washed by age
is heavenly metal flying through infinity.
this cool pure animal of sheer substance
untouched by either vanity or repute
lives, moves, and wishes fast.
by such seasoned discipline
do women recapture their womanhood?
when you stand in silence
you are indeed a creature of God.
now and then I am secretly amazed that
you get prettier and prettier.

January, 1927

innocent tale

Chieko claims there is no sky over Tokyo
and says she longs to see a real sky.
in surprise I look up.
what I see between the young cherry leaves
is that clear sky
of never never separable old acquaintance.
that dull misty scumble over the horizon
is the rosy morning moisture.
gazing far away Chieko says
the blue sky that appears each day
over the crest of Mt. Atatara
is Chieko's real sky.

this is an innocent tale of sky.

May, 1928

kinds cohabiting

———in silence, I handle clay.
———rattling the loom, Chieko weaves.
———a mouse runs for a peanut dropped on the floor.
———a sparrow snatches it away from him.
———a praying mantis sharpens his sickles on the clothesline.
———a fly-catcher spider skips, hops, and jumps.
———a hanging towel romps by itself.
———the mail arrives with a crash.
———a clock takes a nap.
———an iron kettle takes a nap too.
———a hibiscus leaf lolls out its tongue.
———a little earthquake thumps.
with cicadas as accompaniment
from above this throng of kinds cohabiting
a gigantic fireball shines down headlong over the meridian.

August, 1928

beauty's imprisonment

in my pocket, the red touch of tax papers,
in the street with the cold night wind, apart from my radio at last.

the unjustness of selling, buy and become a possessor.
possession is isolation, I deliver beauty into prison, I.

incompatible are the art of forming and the power of money,
incompatible are the joy of making and embittered indolence.

waiting for me in an empty house are Chieko, clay, and chips of wood,
a sweet bun in my pocket is still warm, and crushed.

March, 1931

distant view of life

a bird starts up at my feet
my wife goes mad
my clothes become ragged
the back-sight distance 9000 feet
ah! this rifle is too long

January, 1935

Chieko riding the wind

Chieko gone mad is mute
just signals to blue magpies and plovers
along a windbreak dune
pine pollen from all around flows yellow
blown by the clear May wind,
                    hazy the 99 Mile Beach
Chieko's summer kimono appears and disappears
                    between the pines
there, on the white sand, are truffles
I follow slowly after her
gathering truffles
blue magpies and plovers are Chieko's friends
the terribly clean morning sky is her finest promenade
for Chieko is no longer human
Chieko flies

                              April, 1935

invaluable Chieko

Chieko sees what is invisible,
hears what is inaudible.

Chieko goes to places impossible to go,
does things impossible to do.

Chieko doesn't see corporeal me,
but yearns for the me behind me.

Chieko has abandoned the weight of suffering,
drifted out to an infinitely vast sphere of the aesthetic.

though frequently I hear her voice calling me,
Chieko no longer owns a ticket for the human world.

July, 1937

Chieko playing with plovers

sitting on the desolate sand
of the 99 Mile Beach, Chieko plays.
her many friends call Chieko's name.
Chi Chi Chi Chi Chi.........
leaving their little footprints in the sand
the plovers approach Chieko.
mumbling to herself
Chieko lifts her hands and beckons.
Chi Chi Chi........
the plovers beseech, wanting the clams she holds
and Chieko gently scatters them.
the plovers in flight call to Chieko.
Chi Chi Chi Chi Chi.........
I can see her lonely back
turned on the business of being human
for she has already gone beyond Nature.
far from her, in the sunset over the windbreak
I stand still forever, bathed in pine pollen.

July, 1937

at the foot of the mountain

Mt. Bandai has a back-mountain that slants and splits in two
staring steeply up at the August sky
the mountain-skirts bend and wave
the pampas grass grows wild, burying us deep
my wife gone half mad sits on the grass
leaning heavily on my arms
wailing like an inconsolable child
..........."I'll be a wreck soon"
demon fate has come to kidnap her mind
inescapable parting of her soul
and premonition of its inevitability
..........."I'll be a wreck soon"
the mountain wind touches coldly my hands wet with tears
silently I look into my wife
and recognize there is no way to regain
this wife who clings to me
looking back from the conscious limit for the last time
my heart now splits asunder, falls off
and coalesces with our silent surroundings

June, 1938

34

lemon elegy

you had yearned for a lemon so long
your clean teeth bit fresh
into the lemon taken from my hands
on a sad white light bed of death
a topaz-colored scent arose
a few drops of heavenly lemon juice
suddenly restored lucidity
your blue limpid eyes smiled a little
how healthy your strength was gripping my hands
though there was a storm in your throat
on such a brink of life as this
Chieko became the Chieko of long before
and drained a lifelong love in one moment
then for an instant
drawing a deep breath as once you did
                    on a mountaintop long long ago
your organ stopped
behind a vase of cherry blossoms in front of your picture
today I shall place a cool shining lemon again

February, 1939

to the deceased

getting up at dawn like you, a sparrow pecks on the window
silently like you, Gloxinia blooms by my bedside

the morning wind awakens the person in my body
your odor is cool in the bedroom at 5 A.M.

pushing a white sheet aside and stretching out my arms
I greet your smile in the summer morning sun

you whisper to me what today means
you stand like a person of authority

I become your child
and you my childlike mother

you are there, still there
you become all things and fill me

though I doubt I deserve your love
your love envelops me, ignoring all

July, 1939

plum wine

a bottle of plum wine that dead Chieko had prepared
now looks like a gem congealed in an amber goblet,
enveloping light with dense sediment under a decade's weight.
I think of the woman who left this behind for me
at her death
to drink alone in the cold late night of early spring.
threatened by anxiety from her own deteriorating brain,
saddened by her own impending doom,
Chieko put all her belongings in order.
seven years of insanity ended with her death.
quietly I taste
the fragrant sweetness of this wine found in the kitchen.
even the clamor of the world of storm and stress
cannot violate this moment.
as I stare straight at a wretched life,
the world just hovers, distant and encircling.
the night wind has died away.

March, 1940

Chieko's papercuts

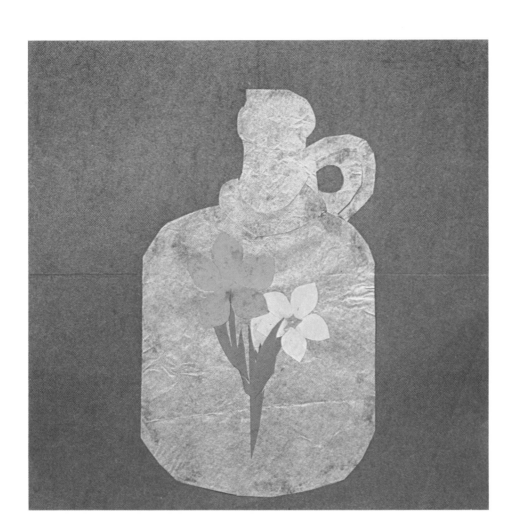

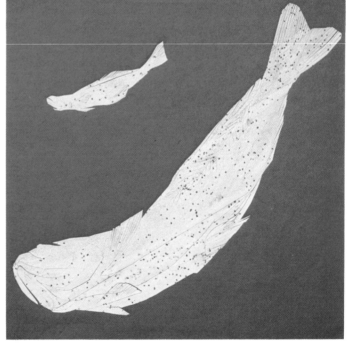

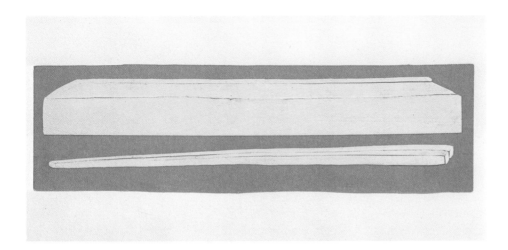

the latter half of Chieko's life

In ten days or so, it will be two years since my wife Chieko died of pulmonary tuberculosis as a schizophrenic patient in Room #15 of James Hill Hospital at Minami Shinagawa in Tokyo. As a result of my encounter with Chieko in this world, I had been cleansed by her true love and rescued from a once "decadent" life, and, as my spirit had been totally dependent on her existence, I received such a severe spiritual blow from Chieko's death that I spent several months in total emptiness, as if I had lost, for a while, even the reason for my artistic creation. When she was still alive, I used to show her my sculpture before I'd show it to anyone else. For me it was an incomparable pleasure to discuss the work with her at the end of a day. Moreover she accepted it wholeheartedly, understood it, and loved it passionately. While walking on the streets, she caressed a little piece of my wood carving kept in her pocket. In this world where she no longer exists, who would accept my sculpture as innocently as she did? For several months, I was tormented by the thought that I had no one to show it to any more. A work of beauty is never born merely from some stale ideology or grandiose racial consciousness. Either of these things might become its main theme or motivation, but for the work to come from the bottom of one's heart and have living blood in it, there must inevitably be an exchange of great love. It could be God's love. And it could, indeed, be the unlimited true love of a woman. There is nothing more encouraging to an artist than the consciousness of having one person who will examine his creation with the eyes of fervent love. There is no better latent power than this to assure the completion of something you want to create. The result of the creation might possibly become a public possession. But usually the creator's mind is already full of the all-encompassing desire to have his creation seen by this one person. I had such a person in my wife Chieko. The feeling of emptiness that I had at the time of Chieko's death was therefore equivalent to a world of nothingness. Even though there were things that I wanted to make, I didn't feel like making them, because I knew that in this world there were no longer those loving eyes to see them. After several months of struggle, a certain accident on a night of the full moon made me feel keenly that Chieko had in fact become a universal being to me through her loss of individual being. From then on I felt Chieko's breathing much closer; she became, so to speak, one who stayed with me, and the sensation that she was someone eternal to me became stronger. Thus I regained a measure of calmness, mental health, and, once again, an incentive to work. Now when I finish a day's work, view the result, and look back saying, "What do you think?" Chieko is there without fail. Chieko is everywhere.

The twenty-four years of her life between her marriage and her death were nothing but a continuous round of love, hardship, devotion to art, contradictions, and the struggle against illness. In such a whirlpool, she succumbed to her fatalistic spiritual predisposition and was completely drowned among the waves, entwined by joy, despair, trust, and abandonment. Though people have often suggested that I write down my memories of her, I did not feel like writing about them till today. With the struggle still fresh in my mind, I could not bear writing even about a little corner of our lives, and the doubt as to whether there was any meaning at all in the reporting of one's private life held me back strongly. But now I will write. I will record the fate of this woman as simply as I can. By recording that in the Taisho and Showa eras there was a woman who, all alone, was distressed, lived, and succumbed in ways I shall explain, let me make a parting gift to that poor woman. Believing that if you know one person ultimately, you know everyone, I presume to take up my pen.

Now, let me look back quietly to recall her and summarize her whole life. To begin with, she was born in 1886 at Urushibara, a suburb of Nihonmatsu, Fukushima Prefecture, Japan, the eldest daughter of the Naganuma family, wine-makers. After graduating from a local high school, she entered the Home Economics Department of the Japan Women's College in Mejiro, Tokyo. During her dormitory life, she began to become interested in Western-style painting, and after her graduation from the college, she got permission from her parents, with difficulty, to stay in Tokyo to study oil painting at the Pacific School of Painting; there she was influenced by the popular artists of the day: Nakamura Tsune, Saito Yoriji, Tsuda Seifu. She also joined the women's liberation movement as advocated at the time by Hiratsuka Raicho, and did a cover painting for the magazine *The Blue Stocking*. It was near the end of the Meiji era, and soon she met me for the first time by way of Mrs. Yanagi Yaeko's introduction; we were married in 1913. After our marriage, she still went on with her study of painting, but gradually began to find herself in the dilemma posed by the demands of art and family life; moreover, because she suffered from pleurisy, she was often bedridden. Later, her father's death and the consequent bankruptcy of her family were an added source of extraordinary mental distress. Soon, she started to show symptoms of insanity, as a result of mental disorder due to the change of life. In 1932, she attempted suicide with Adalin. Fortunately she recovered from the poison, but, despite extensive treatment, cerebral cell disorder progressed step by step, and, in 1935, she was completely seized by schizophrenia. She entered James Hill Hospital in February of the same year, and died there quietly in October, 1938.

Her life was really simple, a purely private life throughout, which did not even approach the socially significant. A short period while she was associated with *The Blue Stocking* saw her only social involvement. Not only did she have no social interests, but she was not even sociable by nature. During her relationship with *The Blue Stocking*, she was widely recognized as belonging to the so-called "new breed of woman" by a certain group of people, and the reason why her name Naganuma Chieko was mentioned frequently by the members of that group was that the gossip-mongers of the time circulated rumors, linked with wild exaggerations, for their own amusement. But it seemed to me that she made her way with rather a taciturn, unsociable, illogical, and passionate personality. The consensus among her girl friends at that time was that it was not easy to talk with Miss Naganuma. Even though I don't know too much about her at that time, Tsuda Seifu wrote somewhere, as I recall, that he had frequently seen her walking with high painted wooden clogs and her long kimono skirt trailing behind. This demeanor and her taciturnity perhaps made people feel that somehow there was a curious enigma about her. Even though she seemed to have been regarded as a romantic woman or a lady of fashion, I imagine that she was actually much more simple and unconcerned.

I admit that I know little about the earlier half of her life. Whatever I know about her is limited to things that happened after my introduction to her. As I was so involved with the present, I did not really care to hear about the past, and even her age I did not know correctly until later years. Her character, on acquaintance, was truly simple and sincere, and her mind was always overflowing with something celestial; she was a woman who seemed to have completely devoted herself to love and trust. Because of her innate determination, she seemed to have forcibly restrained her own emotions within herself, and her manner was gentle, without any frivolity. Sometimes her vigor in riding over herself surprised me, but now I can guess that she only attained this by repeatedly making efforts far beyond her capacity.

Though I did not know then, when I think of it now, it seems that half of her life moved steadily toward the goal of mental illness. There seems to have been no other way out of this life led together with me. Before trying to determine the reason for this, let me try to imagine a thoroughly different sort of life. For instance, suppose that we had not been living in Tokyo, but in her home area, or somewhere else amid rural fields, or that her husband had not been an artist like me, but a man of some other profession who nevertheless understood art, say someone engaged in agriculture and cattle-breeding. She might have lived out a more natural longevity. To that extent, Tokyo was a physically unsuitable place for her. Tokyo's air seemed to her always tasteless, arid and coarse. In the Women's College, due to the encouragement of President Naruse, she seems to have ridden a bicycle, devoted time to tennis, and to have passed a very healthy and spirited girlhood. But after graduation she seems to have been generally not very robust; she was very thin and spent nearly half a year in the country and in the mountains. Even after she began her life with me, she used to go home for a few months every year. She could not maintain her health without occasionally breathing country air. She complained very often that there was no sky over Tokyo, as in my poem titled "Innocent tale". . . .

> Chieko claims there is no sky over Tokyo
> and says she longs to see a real sky.
> in surprise I look up.
> what I see between the young cherry leaves
> is that clear sky
> of never never separable old acquaintance.
> that dull misty scumble over the horizon
> is the rosy morning moisture.
> gazing far away Chieko says
> the blue sky that appears each day
> over the crest of Mt. Atatara
> is Chieko's real sky.
>
> this is an innocent tale of sky.

As I myself was born in Tokyo and raised there, I could not physically feel her urgent distress; I thought that some day she would also adjust herself to her metropolitan surroundings. But her desire for fresh transparent nature remained till her death. Living in Tokyo, she tried to satisfy this desire by many means. Her constant sketching of the weeds growing around the house, studying them botanically, the growing of lilies and tomatoes in the bay window, the eating of raw vegetables, and a passion for a recording of Beethoven's Sixth Symphony—all these things were variations on the attempted fulfillment of this desire; but even regarding this alone, her constant unvoiced pain over half of her life must have been beyond my imagination. The joy she showed on her last day as she held a piece of Sunkist lemon brought by me just a few hours before her death must also have been related to this. Biting the lemon, she looked as if both her body and mind were being washed by the fresh scent and juice. A still greater cause for her final mental breakdown was probably the distress created by the conflict inherent in the opposing demands of her fierce devotion to art and the daily routine based on her pure love toward me. She loved painting passionately. Apparently in college she was already painting in oils, and was always undertaking such projects as the production of backdrops for student performances at their arts festivals. I understand that the reason why her parents finally approved of her becoming a painter, despite their initial objections, was that the ability apparent in the portrait of her grandfather that she had painted at that time positively amazed her family. This painting, which I saw later, had beautiful color values and a simple though subtle harmony. I am not familiar with the paintings she did during the few years after her graduation, but I imagine that they were somewhat sentimental and sweet in mood. She destroyed all of her works from those days without showing them to me. All I could do was imagine them from her rough sketches. After we started to live together, she continued her still-life studies, and painted hundreds of them. Landscape paintings were done in her home province and on her trips to the mountains; figures were done in sketch form, but not executed in oil paintings. She was devoted to Cézanne and naturally received a strong influence from him. In those days, I was also painting in oils in addition to my sculpture; but our studios were separate. She worked hard at color. As she did not hope for merely modest success, she goaded herself on to the point of self-torture. One year she spent her summer at the Goshiki Hot Spring resort near her home province, and came back with paintings of the local landscape. Some of the small pieces were excellent, and she wanted to submit them to the Bunten Exhibition (sponsored by the Ministry of Education); she delivered them with other larger works, but they were not appreciated and were dropped by the jurors. After that, despite my frequent encouragement, she never again tried to submit her works to any exhibition. For an artist I think it is of great spiritual help to appeal to the public and to have a chance to relieve internal congestion through public exhibition of his works; but her having shut herself out of such opportunities might well have helped to increase her spiritual introversion. As she always aimed at the best, she was always dissatisfied with herself, and her works were always unfinished. In fact, I could not deny that the color in her painting was still inadequate. Though her sketches showed amazing power and grace, she could not master the technique of oil painting to the full despite her efforts. This depressed her. Now and then, she shed tears alone in front of her easel. When by accident I came upon such a scene in her studio, I also felt an indescribable sadness and could not say even a word of consolation. You should also know that I was financially in worse shape than you can imagine: only once did I have a maid before the Great Earthquake; otherwise my life was passed only with her, and since both she and I were formative artists, there was considerable difficulty in the adjustment of our time. Once we became involved with our work, we could not eat, clean house, go shopping, etc., and everything else in our life stopped. Such days occurred often, but, after all, she was a woman and was expected to manage the household chores; moreover, if I sculpted in the daytime, at night I had to write articles, very often even sacrificing the time to eat. The more often this happened, the less time *she* had for her painting study. Perhaps a poet might be able to proceed with half of his work mentally, requiring only a part of his time for execution, but in formative art one cannot do the thing without a specific allotment of time. So, you can imagine how much she suffered. She tried at all costs not to cut down my working time, to permit my sculpture to proceed and keep me from the necessity of daily chores. She gradually reduced her oil-painting time and sometimes tried clay sculpture and later started to spin silk, dye it with vegetable pigments, and weave it. Even now I own the home-spun clothes she made. Mr. Yamasaki Takeshi, an authority on Kusakizome (a dyeing method using vegetable pigments), sent me a condolence telegram with the following *waka* poem:

> that elegant woman
> who wove
> a straight blue stripe
> into her sleeve
> has gone, now

Though she did not say so, she had despaired of her oil painting. It couldn't have been an easy affair for her to despair of the art she loved so passionately and regarded as her life work. Years later, on the night she attempted suicide by poison, a basket of fruit just bought at Senbikiya Store was found placed like a still life in the adjacent room, and a new canvas was found standing on the easel. My heart was pained at seeing it. I wanted to cry aloud.

As she was gentle though resolute, she kept everything to herself and moved on in silence. She always gave her best to things. Not only matters of art, but also problems of culture in general and the spirit: she brooded, disapproved of ambiguity, and despised compromise. She was like a string stretched at all times; the brain cells could not hold such extreme tension any longer and were ripped apart. Totally exhausted, she fell. I don't know how many times I was cleansed by this purity of her inner life. Compared to her, I felt myself to be vague and impure. Just from looking at her eyes I always perceived more than a hundred moral lessons. In her eyes was mirrored the sky over Mt. Atatara. When I was making her bust, I felt acutely that her eyes were far beyond my reach, and I was ashamed of my impurity. To think of her now, she seemed to have hidden within her a fate that made it impossible for her to survive safely in this world. So, in seclusion, she lived in a world beyond this earthly air. As I recall, it seemed to me at times that she was a soul only temporarily of this world. She had no worldly greed; her life was sustained solely by her love for me and by art. She was always young. In addition to her spiritual youthfulness, her face revealed extraordinary juvenescence. Whenever I traveled with her, wherever we'd go, people took her for my sister or daughter. That's how young she looked; even near death, at first glance she did not look like a woman over fifty years old. At the time of our marriage, I could hardly imagine her in old age and I once asked jokingly, "Will you ever become an old lady?" I remember that she answered casually, "I'll die before I get old." And so she did.

According to the alienist, an ordinary healthy man's brain can stand considerable severe distress, and almost all who suffer from mental disorder are either born with such a congenital disposition or given such a disposition through accident or disease. Though there seem to have been no mental cases in her family line, her brother, the eldest of the family, was certainly eccentric in his behavior; it was because of this that her family went bankrupt, and he himself became severely ill and died in poverty. But I cannot believe that there flowed in him a strong enough predisposition to be recognized as hereditary. Though I have heard that Chieko's skull had been badly damaged by a stone in her childhood, it healed completely without any malfunctioning afterward, and I don't think that this is related to her disease in later years. When her mind developed irregularities, I was asked by a doctor if I had ever been infected with a certain disease in foreign countries. Not only have I never had such experiences, but when our bloods were tested, the results were always negative. So it would be hard to establish that a predisposition to schizophrenia existed physically in her. But I *can* say that all her tendencies, from the time that I met her, proceeded toward this disease step by step. Even her purity I think was not normal. Once she brooded over something she would often abandon everything else; hers was an uncontrollable temperament, and the intensity and depth of her love and trust for me were almost like those of a baby. I was first moved by her because of this unusual beauty of character. In fact everything about her was unusual. Thus I sang in a poem,

> this is your birthplace,
> world that bore this strange and singular body.

Whether she approached her final breakdown step by step or the illness advanced gradually, inevitably, like a spiral, I did not see it clearly until she had almost reached the last stage. Till that time, I had not the slightest doubt about her mental condition. She seemed, after all, extraordinary but not abnormal. When I became aware of her derangement for the first time, her change of life was nearing.

Let me jot down a few other things I remember about her.

As I mentioned before, the person who introduced Miss Naganuma Chieko to me was

Mrs. Yanagi Yaeko, her senior at the Women's College. She was the wife of Yanagi Keisuke, a painter who had been my friend since my New York period, and was working for the Ofu Group. It was around 1911. I had come back from France in July, 1909. Making a hole in the roof of a retreat house in my father's garden, I converted it into an atelier, where I practiced sculpture and oil painting. I also opened a small gallery called "Rokando" at Awajicho in Kanda and held exhibitions of avant-garde art. Then I joined a new literary movement, the Subaru School, which suddenly burst forth in Japan at that time; simultaneously, my late-sown youth exploded, and I indulged myself in a "decadent" life, in the constant company of Kitahara Hakushu, Nagata Hideo, Kinoshita Mokutaro, etc. With anxiety, restlessness, yearning, despair, I passed through wild days; finally I attempted to relocate to Hokkaido, but failed in this at the outset. This was a time of unpredictable spiritual crises, and perhaps Mr. Yanagi Keisuke, deeply concerned about me, intentionally introduced Chieko to me at such a time. She was extremely graceful, taciturn, equivocal in speech; she usually just looked at my works, drank tea, listened to my tales of French painting, and went home. In the beginning, I did not notice anything but her skillful manner of dressing and her delicate appearance. As she never brought her own paintings, I did not know what she had been painting. In the meantime, I had an atelier built by my father, and upon its completion in 1912, I moved into it alone. She visited me there to congratulate me with a big pot of Gloxinia. Right after the death of the Emperor Meiji, I went sketching off Cape Inubo. At that time, she happened to be staying at another inn with her sister and a friend, so I met her again. Later, she came to stay at my inn, and we walked, dined, and sketched together. We must have looked suspicious: at least one of the inn maids followed behind us to watch our stroll. They suspected that we were about to commit love-suicide. She later told me that if I had asked something unreasonable of her then, she was prepared to jump right into the water to her death. Though I did not suspect any such thing, I was strongly impressed by her innocence, her disinterested simple temperament, and her endless love of nature. Like a child, she enjoyed the shelter-belt woods on Kimigahama Beach. While taking a bath, however, I saw her accidentally in the adjoining bathroom and had a sudden premonition that there was to be a permanent tie between us. She had a truly beautiful body.

Soon she started to send me love letters, and I began to believe that there was no other woman to whom to entrust my heart. Nevertheless, I was afraid that my feeling might be merely temporary. I also warned her. Thinking about my future struggle for a livelihood, I had no desire to involve her in such a mess. At that time, within our narrow circle of artists and women, vicious rumors were circulated concerning us, rumors that put both of us into embarassing situations with our families. However, she trusted me completely; and I worshiped her. The more malicious the remarks we heard around us, the more strongly we were united. Since I was aware of the impure elements and the remnants of my previous life which existed in myself, at times I almost lost all confidence in myself; at such times, she always cast her pure light on something hidden within me, and made it visible to me. I sang in my poem, "To a woman in the suburbs":

> with a child's sincerity
> you discovered my invaluable true self
> in my numerous guises quite defiled
> I know not what you found
> only that when you are the supreme judge
> my heart is rejoiced by you

It was her genuine love that, in the end, rescued me from my desperate and decadent mood.

For two months (August and September) in 1913 I stayed at the Shimizuya Inn in Kamikochi, Shinshu, and painted there some twenty to thirty oil paintings for the Seikatsusha Exhibition that I was to hold with Kishida Ryusei and Kimura Shohachi at the Venus Club in Kanda that fall. At that time, all those who wanted to go to Kamikochi used to cross over Tokugo Pass through Iwanadome from Shimajima, and it was quite some distance. That summer, staying at the same inn, there were Kubota Utsubo, Inokichi Ibaragi, and Mr. and Mrs. Weston who came to climb Mt. Hotaka. In September she came to visit me with her painting equipment. The day when I received notice of her arrival, I went to greet her at the Iwanadome crossing over Tokugo Pass. She came climbing up briskly, having left her luggage to the porter; even the mountain folk were surprised by her untiring legs. I guided her to the Shimizuya Inn, again crossing over Tokugo Pass. As she faced the landscape of Kamikochi, her joy was unbounded. Though she seemed to have some trouble with her pleura even at that time, nothing serious happened to her during her stay in the mountains. I then saw her paintings for the first time. Her style indicated a rather subjective view of nature with some originality, and showed considerable promise. I painted everything that struck my eye—Mts. Hotaka, Myojin, Yaketake, Kasumizawa, Roppyakutake, the Azusa River.... Even in her sickbed in later years, she still looked at one of my self-portraits done at that time. I was asked by Mr. Weston if she was my sister or wife, and when I answered that she was my friend, he grinned. A contemporary newspaper in Tokyo carried an exaggerated article entitled "Love on the mountain" about us at Kamikochi. Perhaps this was based on a rumor brought back by someone who had gone down the mountain. This again upset our families. On October 1, everyone on the mountain went down to Shimajima. The magnificence of the yellow leaves of the *katsura* trees filling a mountain pocket in the Tokugo Pass was unforgettable. She later reminisced about it often.

From then on, my parents worried about me very much. I felt sorry for my mother. Their dreams were all broken. Since I had neither promoted myself in the sculpture world, taking advantage of my "returned-from-abroad" status, nor accepted a teacher's position, nor married a bride from a respectable Tokyo family, I became utterly incomprehensible to my parents. Though I was concerned, in 1914 I nevertheless finally requested my parents to permit me to marry Chieko. In the end they approved. Since we were going to live in the atelier, apart from my parents, I conceded the ownership of all our real estate to my brother and his wife who lived with my parents. We started our household stripped bare. Of course, we could not go to Atami for our honeymoon. For a long time from then on we lived in poverty. Though she had been raised in an affluent, powerful family, or perhaps because of that, she was very careless about money and was little aware of the dreadfulness of destitution. Even when I had to sell my suits to an old-clothes dealer, she just watched casually, and if she found no money in the kitchen drawer, she just did not go shopping. We often wondered if we could make it through, but whenever I said that I had to finish my unfinished works no matter what, she would always agree that my sculpture should never be given up half-done. As we did not have a steady income, when we had money, we were well off, but once it was gone, we were penniless the next day. In all our years together, I only bought her a few kimono. She gradually stopped wearing the ornate kimono of her youth, and finally wore only sweaters and pants at home—which were, nonetheless, very beautiful and becoming. It was around this time that I wrote a poem entitled "You get prettier and prettier":

> when women cast off accessories one by one
> why is it they become so beautiful?
> your body washed by age
> is heavenly metal flying through infinity.

She who did not care about her own poverty was very much hurt by the fall of her family. She had gone home a few times to put their household accounts in order, but in the end they went bankrupt. A big fire in Nihonmatsu Village. Her father's death. The heir's debauchery. Ruin. To her, these must have been unbearably sorrowful events. Though she was often ill, she would always recover completely when she went home. How much the loneliness of having no more home to go back to must have tormented her. Though it was a function of her personality, it was fatal that she did not have many companions to distract her from her loneliness. Staking everything on her love for me, she gradually alienated herself from her school friends. Only Miss Sato Sumiko, who worked for the Agricultural Laboratories in Tachikawa, and a few other friends remained with her. Even they met with her only once or twice a year. When she was at school, she was quite healthy and enjoyed sports to an excessive degree, but after graduation, she always had trouble with her pleura. A few years after her marriage, she was hospitalized with a severe wet pleurisy, and though she fortunately recovered from it completely, later she was hospitalized for a surgical operation on a retroflexion of the uterus resulting from horse-riding. She also suffered from appendicitis and was always sickly. During the latter half of her life, she enjoyed good health for only a few years around 1925. She did not, however, seem moody even when she was ill. She was always serene and gentle. When she was sad, she wept, but soon recovered her composure.

In 1931, when I was traveling in the Sanriku district, the first apparent sign of mental disorder hit her. Though I had never traveled more than two weeks leaving her at home, this time I was gone for a month. According to the account related by her niece, who stayed with her during my absence, and also by her mother who visited her, she seemed to suffer from loneliness and once told her mother that she would commit suicide. It was just then that she was approaching the change of life. On the morning of July 15, 1932 (the year when the Olympics were held in Los Angeles), she did not wake up. After 12 o'clock the night before, she must have taken Adalin; there was an empty 25-gr. bottle of sleeping powders. She was all swollen, round like a little girl, with eyes and mouth closed, lying on the bed face up; she did not wake up, no matter how many times we called her name and shook her. She was breathing but she had a very high temperature. Calling a doctor immediately, we gave her antidotal treatment, notified the police department, and took her to Kudanzaka Hospital. A note was found, but it just expressed her love and thanks to me and apologies to her father. The sentences did not betray the slightest mark of brain disorder. After a month's treatment and nursing, she recovered and came home. For a month or so, she was in good health, but then all sorts of mental disorders became noticeable. So, thinking that travelling might do her good, I took her to the hot springs in the Tohoku district, but when we came back to Tokyo her condition was even worse than it had been before we left. Her condition moved a step forward, a step backward. In the beginning, as she often had hallucinations, she made a sketch of each of them in the notebook lying on her bed. She indicated the moment-to-moment changes in them with time notations. She told me excitedly of their unequaled beauty of form and color. After that period, her consciousness became dim, and I had to give her meals and baths. Both I and our doctor took this to be a temporary phenomenon related to the change of life, and she was moved to the house on 99 Mile Beach where her mother and sister were living and given hormone pills. I visited her once a week by train. In 1934, my father was hospitalized in the University Hospital with a stomach ulcer; after his discharge he died, on the tenth of October. By the seashore Chieko's physical condition improved, emerging from that state of listlessness, but her brain disorder worsened. She played with birds, or became a bird herself, or, standing at a corner of the pine forest, she repeatedly called "Kotaro Chieko Kotaro Chieko" for an hour or so. I took her back to our atelier from the seashore when all the affairs after my father's death were settled, but her physical deterioration accelerated like a locomotive. Her condition was diagnosed by Dr. Morooka, but as she began to behave violently and became too dangerous for home treatment, in February, 1935, we put her in James Hill Hospital in Minami Shinagawa, which a friend had introduced us to. We decided to leave everything to the guidance of Dr. Saito Tamao, the hospital head. And fortunately I had Chieko nursed till her death by her gentle niece, Haruko, who had become a first-class nurse. It is still too painful for me to write about her life and my memories of her in the period after 1932. In the latter half of this hospital life, however, her condition remained comparatively calm, and though her mind was split, her hands seemed to be occupied happily with her cut-paper pictures which accomplished what she had not been able to achieve through oil painting in the past. One hundred or so of these cut-paper pictures constitute a record of her abundant poetry, her life, her joyful creativity, color harmony, humor, and an expression of her delicate compassion. In this art she is alive and truly healthy. For her, the greatest happiness was to show these to me when I visited her. While I was looking at them, she would smile or nod, with true joy. On her last day, while handing the entire collection over to me, she tried to smile faintly through her rough breathing. Her face expressed complete relief. Washed in the scent of a lemon I had brought, she left this world quietly after a few hours. It was the night of the fifth of October, 1938.

December, 1940

atomizing dream

together with Chieko, I took a fancy cable car up
to look down into Vesuvius.
dream is corpuscular like perfume
Chieko enveloped me densely with her twentyish spray.
from the telescope tip made like a slender bamboo pipe
the gaseous fire was gushing out as from a jet plane.
looking through this telescope, I saw Mt. Fuji.
around the basin stood a crowd
as if something bizarre were happening down below.
deep into Vesuvius Chieko threw
an offering of the seven autumnal flora from around Mt. Fuji.
Chieko was fragile, pretty, pure
and full of endless charm.
burning up her female body, limpid as mountain water
leaning on me, she walked over crumbling sand.
the air around was choked with Pompeian scent.
yesterday's disharmony in my whole being vanished
and I awoke in an autumn-fresh mountain hut at 5 A.M.

September, 1948

metropolis

after much meandering, fate has driven me
into that very depth of nature Chieko yearned for.
fate has killed the living Chieko in the city,
instead, placing me, an urban child, here.
the mountains in Iwate are rugged, beautiful, unsullied,
and ruthless, surrounding me.
falsehood and indolence perish in this soil.
naked, reckless, I march ahead
without wasting a moment, like nature.
Chieko resurrects by death,
lives here dwelling in my flesh,
rejoices at being smeared with this wilderness.
kaleidoscopic phenomena of the universe,
the ever-changing ups and downs of generation,
Chieko catches all
that I recognize by touch.
my heart bustles,
and sitting at the fireside of a little mountain cottage
that people call a forest hermitage
alone I feel this is the Earthly Metropolis.

October, 1949

guiding

yes, three mats are enough for us to sleep on.
this is a kitchen.
this is a well.
the mountain water is as delicious as the mountain air.
that field is $\frac{1}{13}$ of an acre,
and it is now the cabbage season.
this open grove is a row of yuccas,
around the hut are chestnuts and pines.
this is a view from the top of the slope,
forty miles open view toward the south
on your left is the Kitakami Mountain Range,
on your right are the Ou Border Mountains,
through the central plain runs vertically the Kitakami River,
around that hazy end
should be the Kinkazan offing.
Chieko, are you pleased? do you like it here?
behind you, the mountain leads to the Poison Woods
where even the antelopes and the bears come out.
Chieko, I bet you'll like this place.

October, 1949

those days

trust in others saves us.
Chieko flatly trusted in me
though I was fairly decadent.
I lost my decadence
when she abruptly plunged inside me.
I was puzzled
to discover something in me
unknown even to myself.
recovering after some slight confusion,
one day I noticed suddenly
Chieko's close-up
sincere   pure   breathless.
strange tears flowed from my eyes,
I faced Chieko anew.
Chieko greeted me with a smile
and enveloped me with her pure sweet odor.
intoxicated with its delicacy I dismissed all.
by the strange power of this celestial woman
who defies even my bestiality
for the first time I, a decadent, found my place.

October, 1949

64

blizzard night monologue

a snowstorm is raging outdoors.
even a rat wouldn't be out on such a night,
the village is dead asleep far away
and not a soul is on the mountain.
throwing a big root into the hearth
I make a towering, glorious fire.
in my bones, now sixty-seven,
I feel much better off now.
as long as I have that desire,
it isn't easy to pursue genuine work.
the depth of the work of art
demands such insentience.
if you haven't got it at all, it's out of the question,
if you have known it well but haven't got it now, it's best.
even if Chieko should reappear now,
I would perhaps just romp around and laugh.
that imperceptible fragrance
from the inside of stern insentience
must be "divine transcendence."
getting senile isn't good either, though.

October, 1949

Chieko the Element

Chieko has reverted to an element.
I don't believe in the self-existence of the spirit.
but Chieko exists.
Chieko is in my flesh.
adhering to me,
phosphorescing in my cells,
frolicking with me,
beating me,
she keeps me from becoming the prey of dotage.
spirit is another name for body.
the Chieko who exists in my flesh
is nothing but the Ultima Thule of my spirit.
Chieko is the supreme judge,
I err when Chieko is dormant within me,
I am right when I hear Chieko's voice in my ears.
Chieko, frolicsome,
romps around my whole existence.
Chieko the Element is still here
within me and smiles at me.

October, 1949

naked form

I long for the naked form of Chieko.
modest and full
solemn like a constellation
undulating like a mountain range
always covered with thin mist
there was a fathomless sheen
to its agatelike formation.
still I remember meaningfully
even a tiny mole on her naked back;
polished by the ages of memory
its whole existence flickers even now.
to create that formation once again
with my hands
is a covenant fixed by nature;
for that purpose, meats are given me
for that purpose, vegetables of the fields are given me
rice, wheat, and butter are permitted me.
leaving the naked form of Chieko in this world
I shall soon return to the elemental core of nature.

October, 1949

to play with Chieko

Chieko is in dimension a.
dimension a is absolute reality.

reality of phantasmal life
as I play with Chieko in the mountains of Iwate.

no difference in Chieko's play,
even when mushrooms grow on the French Plains.

a pint of rice for today's playing at housekeeping.
by a cow's tail I chop the scallions.

doing battle with the foe, the midget mosquitoes,
I entrust my life to a tiny patch of earth.

a stab of gimlet in the ribs,
ceaseless coughs jetting from pulmonary emphysema.

forming is Nature's axis.
sine qua non of the world's existence.

all is a playful stroll over Chieko's dimension a.
as we play, we get a little less vulgar.

November, 1951

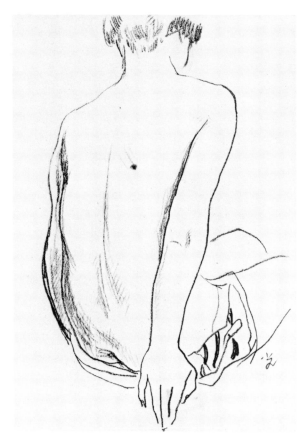

"A Mole" was the title Kotaro gave this drawing of Chieko.

Kotaro in 1911, beside a bust he made of his father.

THE AUTHOR: Takamura Kotaro (1883–1956) was the son of a famous sculptor, Takamura Koun. After his return in 1907 from New York, where he studied sculpture with Gutzon Borglum, and where he read Walt Whitman, he started writing free verse. He spent most of four years abroad in France, where he read such poets as Verlaine, Baudelaire, Rimbaud, and Verhaeren, and was strongly influenced by Auguste Rodin, whose biography he wrote later and whose writings he also translated into Japanese in 1916. In 1914, he published his first collection of poems, *Dotei* ("The Distance"), and in December of the same year he married Naganuma Chieko. *Dotei* established him as a leading modern poet in Japan, with a uniquely vital and solid style. After Chieko died in 1938, he published *Chieko-sho* ("Some Poems on Chieko"), which became one of the most popular volumes of poetry in Japan. He was awarded the Yomiuri Literary Prize for another book of poems, *Tenkei* ("Paragon"), in 1951. He is also greatly respected for some half-dozen other volumes of poetry and translations (Verhaeren's poems, Whitman's diary, a Romain Rolland play, Van Gogh's memoirs), as well as several books of essays on art, poetry, and culture, and also, of course, for his lifelong activity as a sculptor. On April 2, 1956, he died of pulmonary tuberculosis in Tokyo.

THE TRANSLATOR: Soichi Furuta was born in Los Angeles, and raised and educated in Tokyo. In 1948 he returned to America, where he received a B.A. in fine arts from the University of California in 1954. Now vice president of the creative design firm of Stuart, Gunn, and Furuta, he has received numerous design awards. A poet, who has been published in both Japan and America, Mr. Furuta has also translated Eliot's *Waste Land* into Japanese. Since 1968 he has taught a graduate course in advanced design at Herbert H. Lehman College of the City University of New York.